I0108598

mad girl's crush tweet

mad girl's crush tweet

summer jade leavitt

HEADMISTRESS PRESS

PUBLISHER
Headmistress Press
60 Shipview Lane
Sequim, WA 98382
Telephone: 917-428-8312
Email: headmistresspress@gmail.com
Website: headmistresspress.blogspot.com

For another time

contents

(carol)

(Forgot how to talk) (forgot not to look
at your eyes)   (forgot not to look at
your eyes) (forgot that if I looked)
(I would die)   (You're golden)
(you pick at pieces of gold) (stuck
in your teeth) (you're a bird)
(I say *you're a bird)* (You're medicine)
(I'm mistress)   (we only kiss
when we say goodbye)   (You hit
the road) (I leave your hotel room)
(I walk around the city to get lost
in it)   (Up a block) (up a block) (and
one more over)   (I stop)
(You're like my mother) (you give birth to me)
(you give birth to me)   (I forgot that)
(I carry your baby)   (Wouldn't it be great
if I carried your baby)

(this is not fiction) (this is how it goes)

(With someone else's hands in my mouth
I speak to you) (you, hair long and

shirt buttoned up wrong) (unfucked)
(young) (hungry) (sweating to hear the sound

of your own soul) (Back when I was in love
is when I was supposed to die) (right?)

(You would probably hate me) (bitter like this)
(it's so unsexy) (I wish I could undo) (I mean)

(it's unprecedented) (for me to have a voice)
(a mind) (in times like these) (in which

I am also a we) (and we are never alone) /
(we inhabit a body) (that isn't allowed to want) (You

lie untitled) (like all that's real happens in
parenthesis) (there, but under the radar)

(out of view) (both quiet and screaming)
(With someone else's hands

covering my eyes) (like blind leading
blind) (not an alien) (but a bastard) (like

installing reality) (like intellectualizing desire)
(to remain untouched) (untouching) (like my death

drive is holding me hostage) (and wants more
bodies) (More bodies)   (We the unthought

remainder) (We the force that insists
on the void) (hurling into some unspace) (desperately

trying to get a taste) (of something real) (calling
us to ourselves) *(the mindless violence*

of this textual machine) (and singing)
(Always) / (a day) / (away)

(calling the body I cannot see)

(Summoning you)   (like bloody mary in a bathroom
stall)   (summoning you) (when you are long gone)
(don't know where in the world you are)   (Summoning
you)   (in chipped nail polish and sharp edges)
          (summoning you)   (in a long baby blue gown)
(the kind that opens in the back)
                              (summoning you)
(the way you always wanted)   (to be
summoned)   (summoning you
in sentence structure)   (summoning you in dance moves)
(in rotating colors)   (in twinkling melodies
and in hunger)   (summoning
you)   (at a pit stop
in the middle)   (of Pennsylvania)
(I buy something medicinal
and take a sip)

(in apparitions)

(you brush my teeth)   (all four feet
come up off the floor)
(you are washing old words
right out of me)   (letting the
wounds exit)   (you are finding
new ways to communicate)   (in
absence)   (I am fantasizing
about the air)   (the shapes
it makes)

(in courtship)(and combat)

(There is smoke and there is velvet)
(or no) (there is confetti) (An eerie operatic hum

seeps in above our heads) (Many weapons out)
(on the ready) (We: two bodies) (which can be

anything) (Anything) (in a cat's cradle-like weave
around the room) (which can be anywhere)

(Anywhere) (I admire every move) (I say) (I feed
your ego for free) (Your eyes graze

me)   (laser beams that melt me down)
(like plastic,) (make into a mold)   (in which to pour

your   whatever it is) (not-soul)
(Take shape)   (must be mistaken)   (If you

want more compliments)   (although genuine)
(you'll have to pay me)   (I can tell you

what you could get) (for, say, $100)
(This is flirting under capitalism)

(If you want my love)
(you'll have to work for it)

(O daughter dumb it down)

(how can it be)   (me, as both
the mother and father)   (waking up
with the love of words)   (I talk about
gender)   (before I've had coffee) (whimsical
and tailored)   (mutated and aging)
(I am what made me)   (a vision
of disobedience)   (these are touches
that understand)   (there are new ways
of seeing the body)   (mine sticky with tequila)
(salt saliva lime)   (sings Led Zeppelin
at the gay dive bar)   (my uncelebrated dissemination)
(for no one but myself)   (I make what makes me)
(regenerate)   (about face   their own tools
at their own game)   (when they ask me
to ghostwrite their hope)   (I make the old men
cry)   (and drive away in my Jeep)
(that was passed down from generation to
generation)   (they'll cower) (and call me
sir) (one day)   (but now   locked in my
car)   (I am the most academic girl in this parking lot)
(I promise) (I am reading everything)

(we omen)

(This was supposed to be the future)
(high budget *Born in Flames)*   (we still
opposite the dominant body)   (whose hand
is higher) (whose voice) (loud)   (canon)   (whose blood
is thicker than mine)   (we women are weapons,
I think)   (when our bodies become our own) (I think)
(I've got guns, too) (flexing, the emotional muscle)   (the world
is just a circle jerk I think)   (we women)   (no W)
(just an omen) (I think)   (of the regime routinely) (every night)
(an hour before I fall asleep)   (this is   how
we)(stay alive)   (every touch   is a battle
won)   (to take the man down,
you must become him)

Remains

In a class investigating the Anthropocene we
watched an old news reel of a killer whale that
washed up on some shore in Oregon. Local officials

did not know what to do with the body that
would soon begin rotting. They decided the only
possible option was explosives, like, dynamite, like,

blowing up the whale. Particles of dead whale went
everywhere, even crashing into cars and injuring
onlookers   I wonder about the things I find funny

that also, in a way, I am pained by   trying to make sense
of   when I erase information I can find, logically,
where things went wrong   To imagine what I would

do differently   think I have the answers   an alternate
option to offer wouldn't work   even when retrospect
is everything   I never wanted to write about gray areas.

My neighbor   psychologist in training   we were roleplaying
therapy and I was talking about I Love Her, I Love Her Not, and
how it's not even really about Her, how it's really about me,

how I think it's funny, and Faketherapist says "well,
why are you laughing when you've used the word
devastating?"/   when trying to describe the

intimacy that occurred, I always wind up mentioning
ways in which I was cornered, body and soul,
spotlighted, mystified by someone who understood

what I worshipped. What I worshipped   A woman
autovillainizing and aware of wrongdoing, which is cool,
because I'm always looking for someone wicked

to rip my heart out /   is the criminal in question,
essentially, the footprint   the traces that we make,
inadvertently   inadvertent.   Who can still be wholly

aware of a bad idea   like when I sign my name
with my index in the air,   agreeing to the terms and
conditions of an immediate fix, which, I should know

is bound to get messy   shouldn't somebody here
know what they're doing /   It cost me some trouble
the noise of the spark   at first we merely reduced

that spark   after many attempts, I destroyed
without injuring the action.   This is the case
we've taken on together. /   Faketherapist (and never

real one) explains   erase the information   logically
I can find where things went wrong   "Women can be
bad, too"   nobody here knew what they were

doing   shouldn't somebody here know
what they're doing   We just wanted to see
something explode

(carol too)

(I wanted to write a poem that would
make you proud of me)   (Like intelligence
I hold you above everything else)   (A counterfeit
and fashioned family)   (tied together by
pink satin scarves)   (in bows around our
necks) (we're alike) (alike in the eyes)   (a look
cold enough to freeze eyelashes)   (Maybe
it's kinship)   (there was a word for it)   (I couldn't
find it)   (when something is real) (it leaves
a trace)   (I trace your name) (into my leg
with my finger so I can feel you)   (You taught me
a language I still cannot speak)   (I owe you)
(I owe you my firstborn)   (On the shortest day
of the year) (you called me family)   (You didn't know
what else to call me)   (There was a word
for it)   (you couldn't name it)   (You wanted
a child) (but you got me instead)

(the erasure of a name)

(A Killer) (like death
dances too long
into the light)   (blind)
(you open) (into the light)
(like a mouth) (wide)
(You've never seen
what they do) (with silence) (how
it gets hushed)   (even smaller)
(than when it was born)
(The sound of violence)
(a song) (with your name
on it) (you speed
into speech)   (you don't belong)
(the earth is trying
to eat you)   (faster)
(than you can get a word
out) (Even memories)
(become open mouths)

(where there is no cemetery) (for affairs)

(she said to me)   ("go mourn")
(I followed suit)   (there is smoke in the
air)   (I am jumping
to conclusions)   (delusional) (from
the day I was born) (read: Aries)   (we cut
a deal)   (when you bleed)(I bleed)
(but we grieve)   (grave, we became)
(lipstick into stone) (silver slipping)(glitter)
(flying too close to the sun)   (streaming)
(down my face again)   (like tears, but
prettier)(I guess you must be dead to me)

(it goes down with us looking fabulous) (and eating french fries)

(I eat 5 or 6 years) (for breakfast)
(this shouldn't be hard)   (We are given

that doomsday clock) (to watch it all)
(come full stop)   (Armageddon was sexy)

(especially when we couldn't see) (now
we walk into anything)   (that looks like a womb)

(Isn't the point of the end)   (that you're always arriving)
(instead)   (something like a sci-fi sequence)   (we bleed

through the night)   (in your high top truck)(from Texas,
floor glittered)   (with red bull cans)   (we go hunting

for something)   (that will bring us closer together)
(always arriving)   (ready to be carried into a new world)

(we sit sixth in line)   (at a Wendy's drive through)

(In a Realm that Doesn't Exist)

Some man was snapping photos of us
kissing each other even as he sat

in the back seat of the car he was being driven
away in   that Jesus fish decorating the

bumper   I said in jest "he's taking pictures to
have proof that we belong in hell,   you know

because God can't see what goes on
underneath awnings" /   I'd rather take the swing

at myself first   It's the dizzying vortex   egos
eat egos   we cannibalize our own kind   that's why

we all talk about the same things   dyke bars,
farmers markets, haircuts, hunger, *The Well of*

Loneliness, The Price of Salt, and   "If a molotov
cocktail doesn't come through my door   we'll be

here for twenty-plus years" /   *the desire to see*
is the manifestation of the desire to be seen

and we're always being shown what we look like
dying on TV /   If I'm going to hell

I'm also tricking myself   into a different realm
in which I believe in the poetic mistake

I made   when the time on my phone
set to two minutes ahead   /   The cynicism

it's intrinsic   I'm picturing post-apocalyptic
but *it matters what thoughts we think*

other thoughts with   I'm trying
to imagine what the future for us would even look like

(re: Bound)

(You are drawing my name
on a chalkboard)   (I am taking
your heart)   (and putting it next
to my name)   (you are shifting
in your seat)   (I am on
a plane)   (you are lost)   (you are
somewhere foreign)   (I am busy
working)   (reading between the
lines)   (seeing your name daily)   (I
am climbing manifestation)   (yeah
two ladies)   (we can make
babies)   (reproducing our own
images) (in the back of each
other's imaginations)   (until there
are 100 copies of my face)   (burned
into the back of your brain)

(i'm in luv w/ a cyborg)

(in the market at night)   (you play a trick) (something spills
and)   (we malfunction)   (in the produce aisle) (we fuck
right next to the lettuce)   (wet dreams) (are 70% water)   (you
know, just like the body)   (can you believe)(I'm still waiting
to become real?)   (I love you) (Being-in-Machine)   (there
is a certain kind of vertigo)   (you affect-on-me)   (a secure
destruction) (I can trust)   (we feel through
the wires)   (Screen-touch me)
(I want to be real) (so bad)

(she says "be my mirror")

(the play begins)   (there's little difference)
(between us already)   (between a flame)

(and a touch) (brightness turned up)   (I say)
(this message has no body) (combined fragments)

(make me a hot tragedy) (accessible) (a spectacle)
(two reflections bouncing off of one display) (I say)

(what's the difference in doubles)   (copies)
(two black leather jackets) (noses   bone structure)

(matching haircuts)   (and parroting tongues)
(she becomes the one she loves)   (down to

the molecules)   (in her mouth)
(she carries my pain) (to repeat on street corners)

(reperformed)   (in perfect sync) (I sip
my sparkling water)   (it accompanies

what's left of me and)   (pedestrians take
the pieces) (she gives away)

(autoquasi)

There is something in my body   something
other than blood   it is not my own   into it
time slips   opens doors for strangers   carries
poison in the large pores of my face   comes out
after midnight crying like agave   when it waits
one full decade to flower and then just   /   I call it
phantom penetration   when I forget my own
senses   when I cannot talk about the pain without the pain
recreating itself   /   when do you know something
you've created is complete   when is it okay
to reperform your trauma   when we are trying to heal
/ I don't want to hurt anyone   I want to be a forgotten
product   and let myself slip into the time slipping /
in real life I have no words   I only have the words given
to me   I mean   it is all one wound   to reject
this wound would take   the body rejecting itself   swishing
salt water   constantly   creating new language   I am
almost my own   singing to the pain like it is a baby

(i love being a millennial)

(I love my 2002 Britney Spears pencil pouch)
(Saturday morning music video countdowns)
(all things bright and flashy)
(I love killing industries)
(watching corporations crumble)
(I love my horoscope) (discourse) (awareness)
(the 15 year olds giving me skincare tips on Instagram)
(the improvement in alternative meat products)
(covering my webcam with tape)
(knowing our phones are homing devices) (recording everything we say)
(I love my queerness) (and I loved falling in love with my older cousins friend)
(a Gen X-er)
(I loved getting into 80's ballads because of her)
(scanning the radio for Bonnie Tyler)
(and being nostalgic for a time I never knew)
(there are so many different worlds)
(I love watching iGeneration protest)
(I love seeing 11 year olds give speeches)
(and 9 year olds start chants at the March for Migrant Children)
(I love watching old powers fall and better ones organize)
(I love a world with clean water)
(I love a world with free healthcare)
(I love a world with no borders)
(where white supremacists have no power) (died off)
(I love a world where we survive)
(in trying, I think) (maybe if I write it down enough)
(it will come true)

(summoned)

(coming forth)   (came forth)
(from under heavy felt curtains)   (as if)
(a revelation)   *(a priori)*
(so sorry)   (so sweaty)
        (I'm nervous)   (you are
coming forth)   (came forth)
        (from under heavy felt curtains)
(in motion)   (transformed before
my eyes)   (like wine left out
for Elijah)   (that cup
of doubt)   (so sorry) (for what
I've done to you)   (I just wanted
to be wicked, too)   (I summoned) (like
when you press the button)   (for the nurse
to come)   (so sorry) (I thought
you up so hard)
(I thought you up so hard)
(I'm a prophet)

notes & acknowledgments

(this is not fiction, this is how it goes) features quotes and references from Lee Edelman's *No Future: Queer Theory and the Death Drive.*

(we omen) names Lizzie Borden's 1983 feminist sci-fi film "Born in Flames."

(In a Realm that Doesn't Exist) pulls the quote "If a molotov cocktail doesn't come through my door we'll be here for twenty-plus years" from an article about the disappearance of lesbian bars.

"It matters what thoughts we think other thoughts with" is pulled from a larger quote from Donna J. Haraway's book *Staying with the Trouble: Making Kin in the Chthulucene.*

Variations of these poems have appeared on Poets.org ("Carol") and in *The Oakland Review* ("Carol", "Remains", "This is Not Fiction, This is How It Goes", "Carol Too")

Many thanks to Ching-In Chen, Mary Meriam, Risa Denenberg, Headmistress Press, The Academy of American Poets, Lauren Shapiro, Maya Zane Kaisth, Kasem Kydd, Jenna Houston, Adrienne Cassel, Alex Lewis, Starr Jasmine, Robin Leavitt, Bobby Leavitt, Dempzil Chavian, Jaz Elieth Alvarado, Kevin Brophy, Anna Azizzy Rosati, Edith & Theodore Baxter, and Tom Wyroba, for all the ways they have supported, read, listened, guided, and made me think about language to make these poems possible.

about the author

summer jade leavitt is an artist and poet from Miami, FL. She earned her BFA in Fine Arts (with concentrations in Performance, Contextual Practice, and Critical Theory) from Carnegie Mellon School of Art, where she was the winner of the 2018 Academy of American Poets prize. Both her writing and art making practices focus on queer time/futurism, quantum feminism, and deconstructing language and perceptions of reality; she is imagining better worlds, possible bodies. This is her first chapbook. Her website can be found at www.leavittsummer.com

Headmistress Press Books

She/Her/Hers - Amy Lauren

Spoiled Meat - Nicole Santalucia

Cake - Jen Rouse

The Salt and the Song - Virginia Petrucci

mad girl's crush tweet - summer jade leavitt

Saturn coming out of its Retrograde - Briana Roldan

i am this girl - gina marie bernard

Week/End - Sarah Duncan

My Girl's Green Jacket - Mary Meriam

Nuts in Nutland - Mary Meriam, Hannah Barrett

Lovely - Lesléa Newman

Teeth & Teeth - Robin Reagler

How Distant the City - Freesia McKee

Shopgirls - Marissa Higgins

Riddle - Diane Fortney

When She Woke She Was an Open Field - Hilary Brown

God With Us - Amy Lauren

A Crown of Violets - Renée Vivien tr. Samantha Pious

Fireworks in the Graveyard - Joy Ladin

Social Dance - Carolyn Boll

The Force of Gratitude - Janice Gould

Spine - Sarah Caulfield

Diatribe from the Library - Farrell Greenwald Brenner

Blind Girl Grunt - Constance Merritt

Acid and Tender - Jen Rouse

Beautiful Machinery - Wendy DeGroat

Odd Mercy - Gail Thomas

The Great Scissor Hunt - Jessica K. Hylton

A Bracelet of Honeybees - Lynn Strongin

Whirlwind @ Lesbos - Risa Denenberg

The Body's Alphabet - Ann Tweedy

First name Barbie last name Doll - Maureen Bocka

Heaven to Me - Abe Louise Young

Sticky - Carter Steinmann

Tiger Laughs When You Push - Ruth Lehrer

Night Ringing - Laura Foley

Paper Cranes - Dinah Dietrich

On Loving a Saudi Girl - Carina Yun

The Burn Poems - Lynn Strongin

I Carry My Mother - Lesléa Newman

Distant Music - Joan Annsfire

The Awful Suicidal Swans - Flower Conroy

Joy Street - Laura Foley

Chiaroscuro Kisses - G.L. Morrison

The Lillian Trilogy - Mary Meriam

Lady of the Moon - Amy Lowell, Lillian Faderman, Mary Meriam

Irresistible Sonnets - ed. Mary Meriam

Lavender Review - ed. Mary Meriam